F

S

Please return on or before the latest date above.
You can renew online at *www.kent.gov.uk/libs*
or by telephone 08458 247 200

CUSTOMER SERVICE EXCELLENCE

Libraries & Archives

Kent
County
Council

00884\DTP\RN\07.07   LIB 7

FRANKLIN WATTS
LONDON•SYDNEY

Everyone needs friends.

A friend can be someone who is like you or someone with memories to share.

A friend is someone you feel happy with.
You like doing the same things together.
Maybe you agree about what
you don't like too!

What do you like to do with your friends?

Try this later

Draw a picture of you and your best friend,
whoever it might be.

A real friend helps you with a problem. It's easier to sort things out with someone else.

Can you remember a time when a friend helped you out?

Friends talk things over.
A good friend can keep a special secret.

Friends can have quiet times together, too.

9

Friends are always pleased to see you. Sometimes they have a special way of showing how they feel.

How do your friends know that you are happy to see them?

Friends remember when it is your birthday.

How do you make sure you remember your friends' birthdays?

Try this later

Make a special birthday card to give to a friend.

Sometimes friends get angry
with each other.

But they soon make up and
are friends again.

Some people seem to have
lots of friends.
Some people like to have
one special friend.

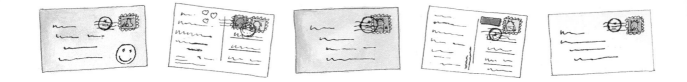

Sometimes friends live far apart.
But they can still talk to each other or
send special messages.

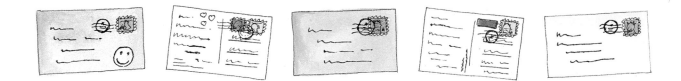

Try this later
There are lots of ways to keep in touch.
Try making a tape-recording to tell
someone all about the things you do.

Friends like to share their favourite things.

They take turns and try to be fair.

Friends have fun together!

Index

This edition 2003
Franklin Watts
96 Leonard Street
London EC2A 4XD

Franklin Watts Australia
45-51 Huntley Street
Alexandria NSW 2015

Copyright © Franklin Watts 1996
Editor: Sarah Ridley
Designer: Nina Kingsbury
Illustrator: Michael Evans

ISBN: 0 7496 5223 3

A CIP catalogue record for this
book is available from the British
Library.

Dewey Decimal Classification
Number: 302.3

Acknowledgements:
The publishers would like to
thank Carol Olivier, Osbert
Clements and Liane Bates of
Kenmont Primary School for
their help with the cover of
this book.

Photographs:
Bubbles 4, 9, 12, 18, 20;
Robert Harding Picture Library 10;
Peter Millard cover; Trip 17;
ZEFA 3, 15.

Printed in Malaysia